Monkeys

by Jo Windsor

T0351217

Contents

Monkey facts

In cartoons, monkeys are shown as little brown animals that chatter, eat bananas and hang from branches by their curly tails.

In the real world, things can be very different!

△ A family group of long-tailed macaques

◁ A Geoffroy's spider monkey

▽ **A wild tamarin monkey**

▲ **A spider monkey at the top of a tree**

- Monkeys are **vertebrates**.
- Monkeys are **mammals**.
- Monkeys' eyes face forwards.
- Some monkeys have 32 teeth; others have 36 teeth.
- Most monkeys have fingernails.
- Most monkeys have thumbs.
- Monkeys live in family groups.
- Monkeys are expert climbers.
- Some monkeys are good swimmers.

All sorts of monkeys

Monkeys come in many colours – some have bright red heads; others have blue and red faces and blue and violet bottoms; some have golden hair.

▶ The Zanzibar red colobus is an Old World monkey

Old World monkeys come from Africa and Asia. They have thin noses with nostrils close together. New World monkeys come from Central and South America. They have flat noses with nostrils set wide apart.

⬤ The red Uakari monkey is a New World monkey

▼ The long-tailed macaque uses its tail for balance

Some monkeys have tails, some don't. Of those monkeys with tails, not all can use them to hang from branches.

Monkeys are all very different from one another!

Big and Small

The pygmy marmoset measures no more than 15 centimetres, and is the smallest monkey in the world. Its hands are too small to grasp most branches, so it has claws to cling to the bark.

⬤ A pygmy marmoset uses its claws to cling to bark

⬤ Barbary macaques grooming themselves

Barbary macaques spend most of their time on the ground. They have large thumbs, which help them to pick up food, and to groom themselves and each other.

The male proboscis [say: pro-boss-kiss] monkey has the biggest nose of all monkeys. Some males have a nose up to 17 centimetres long, which hangs over their mouth. The females have shorter noses, and theirs are upturned. A big nose is a sign of maturity. Females are attracted to males with the biggest noses.

▼ A male proboscis monkey

The black-handed spider monkey

The black-handed spider monkey has four long fingers on each hand, with fingernails at their tips. However, unlike most monkeys, it has no thumbs. This means that it does not grasp branches the way other monkeys, or humans, do. It swings from branch to branch using the **palms** of its hands.

Like many New World monkeys, the spider monkey has a long, **prehensile** tail. The tip of the tail is hairless and the monkey uses this like a fifth hand to grip branches.

▼ The black-handed spider monkey uses its prehensile tail to grip branches

Family life

Monkeys are very **social** animals. Most live in family groups of various sizes. These groups are called **troops**. The **structure** of some troops is very simple – others have a **hierarchy**.

▶ **A troop of baboons on the move**

▶ **Baboons have very close family groups**

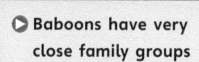

Baboons live in large troops. There are often around 50 males, females and young in one troop. Some troops may have up to 200 baboons!

Friendship is very important to baboons. They spend a lot of time grooming each other, and this keeps the friendships going. They also share food, and defend each other against predators.

The females stay very close to each other and different generations of their **offspring** stay in the same troop with their mothers all their lives.

Black and white colobus monkeys

Black and white colobus monkeys live in small family groups, too. When males are old enough, they leave to form new groups.

Babies are born white, and develop adult colouring at three to four months old. All family members help to care for the babies.

▶ **An eastern black and white colobus monkey with its baby**

Proboscis monkeys

Proboscis monkeys live in groups of up to 20.
These groups may be all-male, or a male with
females and young. To keep his group together
in the **dense** forest, the adult male makes a
'kee honk' sound through his nose.

⬓ A troop of vervet monkeys foraging for food

Vervet monkeys

Vervet monkeys live in groups of up to 70 individuals. During the day, they wander around their **home ranges** in search of food. Their favourite food is fruit, but they also eat leaves and grasses. Most of their time is spent on the ground. At night they sleep in large acacia trees.

Spider monkeys

Spider monkeys live in small family groups, or several families may come together to form groups of 30 or more.

▼ A family group of Colombian black spider monkeys

Barbary macaques

Barbary macaques live in groups of up to 70 or more. During the day they **forage** on the ground, in trees and along stream banks. At night the monkeys form sleeping groups of two or three, with adult males and females in separate groups.

▼ **A sleeping group of Barbary macaques**

▽ A group of
young Japanese
macaques

Japanese macaques

Japanese macaques live in groups
of between 30 and 200. There is
a strict hierarchy amongst both
males and females.

△ Red howler
monkeys

Red howler monkeys

Red howler monkeys live in groups
which may consist of one male and
several females, or many males and
females. Some males live alone.

Mandrills

Male mandrills lead small family groups on foraging trips through the forest. Sometimes, many groups come together and there may be more than 100 mandrills in one place.

Males have long **canine teeth** that they display to warn off other males. They may also bare their canines to family members as a show of **dominance**.

▶ **A male mandrill baring its canine teeth**

Golden lion-tamarins

Golden lion-tamarin monkeys live in small groups. They forage together in the branches of their forest habitat during the day. At night they sleep in hollows in the trees.

▽ **A family of golden lion-tamarins**

△ A black bearded saki and its baby

Bearded sakis

Bearded sakis live in groups of up to 30 individuals. They stay close together as they travel along tree branches to find food. Adult monkeys often hang by their feet to reach hard-to-get food. At night the group finds a sheltered spot to sleep, high in the trees.

Monkey behaviour

Monkeys are very intelligent, so they are able to learn and **adapt**. We can see this by the way they **communicate** with each other, and how they use their **environment**.

Finding food

Capuchin monkeys are famous for using stones to crack open palm nuts.

▶ **A tufted capuchin getting his dinner**

Pygmy marmosets use their long
incisor teeth to make holes in the
bark of trees so that **sap** bleeds
out. They visit the holes each day
to eat the sap, and make new
holes to keep up their food supply.

A winter treat

Many years ago, scientists noticed that a group of Japanese macaques had **extended** their home range into a mountain forest. The monkeys had discovered hot **springs** there. Ever since, these monkeys have been soaking in the warm pools every winter.

▼ Japanese macaques enjoying the hot spring water

When scientists threw wheat onto a sandy beach to feed the macaques, one female worked out how to separate the wheat from the sand. She picked up a handful, and threw it into a pool of water. The sand sank and the wheat floated. Soon, all the monkeys were doing the same.

Watch out!

Snakes, eagles and **carnivores**, such as hyenas, **prey** on vervet monkeys. When a monkey spots one of these predators, it gives a warning call.

◀ A hooded Cape cobra

▽ A Cape crowned eagle

△ A spotted hyena

This call tells every monkey in the group which predator has been spotted. When they hear the 'snake' call, they look on the ground. When they hear the 'eagle' call, they look up. When they hear the 'carnivore' call, they climb into the trees.

Noisy neighbours

Red howler monkeys make a sound like a roar when they communicate with each other. Their calls are some of the loudest sounds made by any animal that lives on land.

When they call, their throats swell like balloons and they produce so much sound that they can be heard several kilometres across the forest. The sound is made by air which is forced through a special bone in the monkey's throat, making it very loud.

Howler monkeys probably call so that they can warn other troops that they are nearby. This helps to avoid fighting between different troops.

▼ A red howler monkey
calling

Quiz

1 Where do Old World monkeys come from?

a Australia

b Africa and Asia

c South America

2 What colour are black and white colobus monkeys when they are born?

a black

b brown

c white

3 What do some Japanese macaques like to do in winter?

a go ice skating

b make snowballs

c soak in pools of warm water

4 Which type of male monkey has the biggest nose?

a proboscis

b pygmy marmoset

c mandrill

Answers on page 31

Glossary

adapt	change
canine teeth	strong, pointed teeth
carnivores	animals that eat meat
communicate	pass on information
dense	thick
dominance	control
environment	surroundings
extended	stretched or made larger
forage	collect or search for
hierarchy	order in a group
incisor teeth	used for cutting or tearing food
mammals	animals that have hair and produce milk
offspring	young of a person, animal or plant
palm	underside of the hand
prehensile	able to grasp
prey	animal hunted by another animal
home ranges	areas used by animals to live in
sap	juice in a plant or tree
social	living with others in an organised group
springs	places where water 'springs up' from under the ground
vertebrates	animals that have backbones

Index